Adventure Life

A Life of Freedom With the Ones You Love

ADVENTURE LIFE: A Life of Freedom With the Ones You Love

For information, contact One Peace Books, Inc.

TEXT . . . . AYUMU TAKAHASHI
DESIGNER . . . . ANNE LOCASCIO
EDITORS . . . . YOUHEI TAKIMOTO, RYO IJICHI
TRANSLATOR . . . . MICHELLE DOSTER
TREASURER . . . . AKIRA NIHEI

© Photos
Pages: Cover,
2, 3, 8-17, 20, 22, 24, 54, 118, 126, 136, 137, 140-144, 146, 148, 150, 154-158, 161, 166, 168, 170-172, 174, 176, 178, 180, 183-188, 192, 202, 203, 210, 218, 222-224, 226-228, 230-233
© Voller Ernst / Mega Press Japan

Pages:
4, 5, 32, 66, 67, 70, 71, 77-107, 110-113, 138, 152, 190, 191, 194-196, 199, 200, 206-208, 212, 213, 215-217, 234, 235, 238-240
© Ayumu Takahashi

Pages: 64, 65, 220, 221
© Sayaka Takahashi

Pages: 119-125
© Takeshi Ijima

Published by
ONE PEACE BOOKS, INC.
57 GREAT JONES STREET
NEW YORK, NY 10012 USA
TEL 212-260-4400
FAX 212-995-2969
www.onepeacebooks.com

Printed in Canada
ISBN: 1-935548-05-0
978-1-935548-05-8

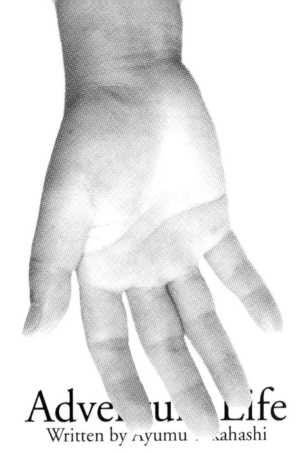

Adventure Life
Written by Ayumu Takahashi

"LOVE & FREE"

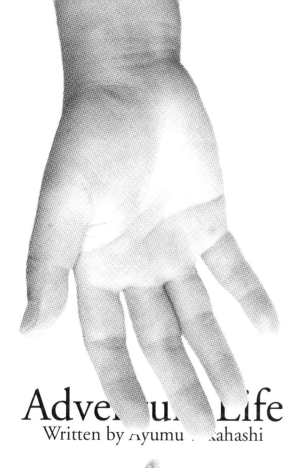

Adventure Life

Written by Ayumu Takahashi

"LOVE & FREE"

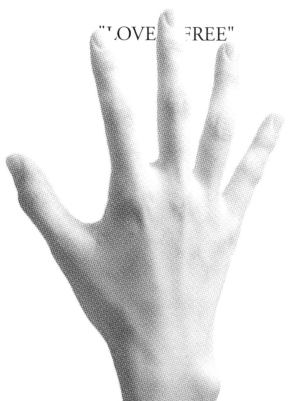

Prologue

From the editor

This book contains the entire story of a thirty-eight-year-old man, Ayumu Takahashi, a free spirit.

It includes everything from opening a bar with friends, starting his own publishing company, taking a trip around the world with his wife, to starting up a village on a remote island in Okinawa.

Recorded here are his actions and the emotions he felt throughout his twenties, always being true to his heart.

With friends, parents, siblings, and his dearest wife and children...
together with the people he loves....

A life of freedom.

This book is filled with such emotion.

Adventure Life
- A Life of Freedom With the Ones You Love -

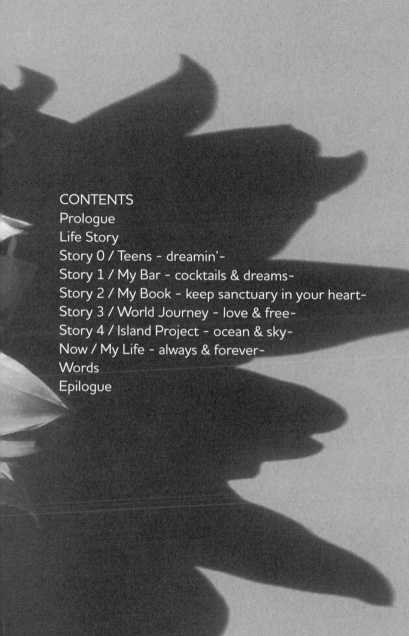

CONTENTS

with friends...

with family...

with wife & children...

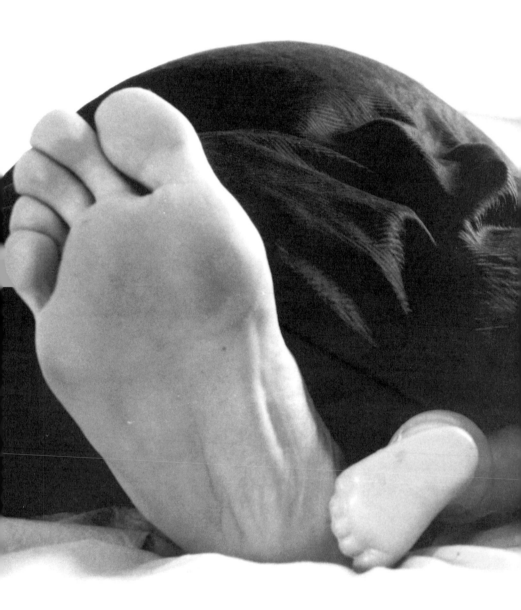

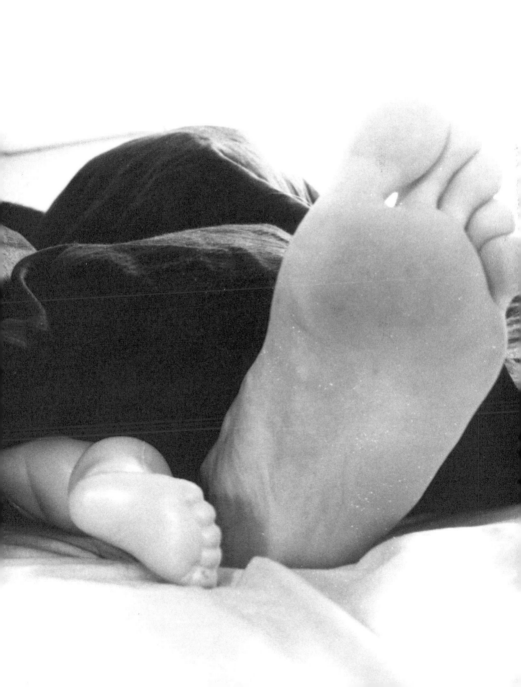

life is a journey
with love & freedom...

A Life of Freedom
With the Ones You Love

Ayumu Takahashi's

Life Story

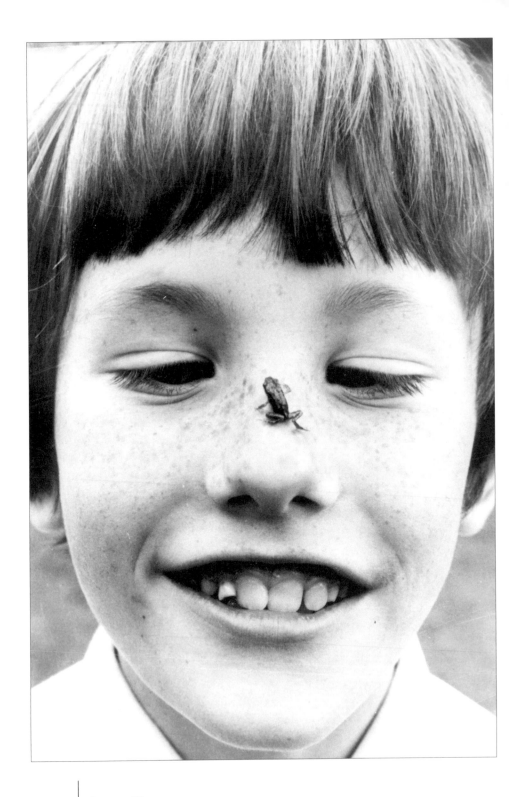

adventure life 高橋 歩

I am Ayumu Takahashi. I was born on August 26, 1972 and am thirty-eight years old.

I was born in Tokyo, raised in Yokohama, and I now live in Okinawa with my wife and son.

For ten years after I turned twenty years old, I gave my all to everything I wanted to do.

Starting my own bar, my own publishing company, traveling around the world with my wife, and building a village on a remote island in Okinawa...

With tears, with laughter, and always with drinks.
I have lived many dreams with my friends and with my beloved wife.

And now, I am here.

This is the story of the ten years of Ayumu Takahashi's twenties.

Let's begin.

STORY 0

TEENS

~ dreamin' ~
Teens—Let's try everything

So, let's start with when I was a kid.

As a kid in elementary school, with both parents as teachers, I was your average baseball-loving kid who grew up having a healthy, happy childhood.

What changed such a refreshing boy was the manga about hoodlums, "Be-Bop High School," that I read in the seventh grade. After I read this manga, my mind was overtaken instantly.

"Cool! This is it! Guys are hoodlums!" Suddenly, it was a 180 degree turnaround.

Immediately, I got my hands on "violation-of-dress-code school uniforms" from some hoodlum upperclassmen, dyed my hair, stepped on the backs of my shoes like hoodlums should...and a so-called hoodlum was born. ☺

At train stations and arcades, if I made eye contact with guys from other schools, I'd yell one hundred percent of the time, "Huh? Punk! Whatcha lookin' at? You want a piece?" But in reality, I was a weak fighter. ☺ Though I pretended to be a real tough guy and bluffing the talk, I remember I was always saying to myself inside, "If possible, I hope this doesn't turn into a fight."

While I played the part of a hoodlum in school saying, "Gimme a break. I can't sit and listen to this lecture," yet, I was the type who would sit and study the *Shinken Zemi* cram school material alone at home. ☺ My tutor from cram school and I were best friends. I even collected the point stickers. Now that I think about it, I was quite nerdy.

And so it was like this—hoodlum by day, nerd by night—that I finished junior high and went on to high school, where I enjoyed myself still being the half-hearted hoodlum. The next turning point for me came during my senior year of high school. Yes, the thing they call guidance counseling.

All of a sudden, I was asked, "What are your plans after graduation?"

I was seriously stumped. I mean, how would I know how to answer something that came straight out of the blue? "What are you going to do? You need to decide right away and start preparing!" The guidance counselors started attacking me. I was completely desperate.

At that time, there wasn't a university or vocational school that I wanted to attend, but I also didn't want to immediately find employment. I didn't have a dream or a desired profession in the first place.

The more I thought about it, the more confusing it became. For the first time, I sat alone in my room listening to Ozaki Yutaka, Nagabuchi Tsuyoshi, BOOWY, and Blue Hearts (inspirational artists of the Japanese youth), and stressed about "a way of life."

While playing my guitar and shouting Nagabuchi Tsuyoshi's "My life is..." in my room, my mom would rush in and ask, "Ayumu, are you all right? Is something troubling you?" ☺

At any rate, at nineteen, I had no clue as to what I wanted to do. But most teens don't have a clear idea of what they want to do, right? I was studying for the college entrance exams in such a state, without a clue, with no motivation. If I tried too hard under pressure, I would get a stomach-ache...

In the end, I took the university entrance exams, but wasn't accepted to any. And so I was plunged into the life of studying to make the next year's cut. It was that common path in life.

During that time, what changed the course of my life was a commercial for Marlboro cigarettes. I saw the image of a cowboy riding through the wilderness on horseback with the huge sunset in the background, the wild and rough work of rounding up wild cattle and thought, "Oh my God! Cowboys are cool! A real man is a cowboy!" ☺

"I have to go to America and learn to become a cowboy!"
It was so very simple, but I felt as though I had a dream for the very first time.

So, first of all, I needed the funds to go to America, and immediately I started working the night shift at a local convenience store. I saved around 200,000 yen working five nights a week for about two months, and then I went to the local travel agent and bought my ticket. My trip to America was final. Of course, I explained to my parents that I had a good reason to go. "English is an important subject on the entrance exams. I'm going to go study English in America," I explained and got their approval. ☺

And then I was in America. I flew into LA on the west coast and crossed the country to Washington D.C. on the east coast, desperately looking for a cowboy. But regardless of where I went, I never encountered a real cowboy like that out of the Marlboro commercial. No matter how many locals I asked, they would reply, "Cowboys? What era are you talking about? To find a real cowboy in America would be like finding a samurai in Japan," or "Cowboys? Oh, no!" ☺

In the end, I gave up. Discouraged, I had no choice but to return to Japan. After all my efforts of chasing the first real dream I had, my ship was sinking. I was so depressed on the flight home.

It was yet another manga, *Jyun Bride*, that lifted my spirits after my cowboy dream had been shattered and I had lost all motivation. This manga is by Satoshi Yoshida, who also wrote one of my favorites, the awesome *Shonan Bakusouzoku*. Anyone who has read this and says they don't want to shack up with someone is lying. After reading this, I got all worked up and thought, "I want a live-in girlfriend." ☺

And that is when I realized the shocking truth that "Hey, if I get accepted into college and move out on my own, I can live with someone!" I was missing the key person, a partner, but...I was very optimistic thinking, "Well, if I can move out on my own, it'll all work out." From that point on, I concentrated on studying for the entrance exams. Clear and simple! Because I am originally the type to put all my energy into something as long as the goal is defined, from that point on, my grades went up and I was accepted in the spring.

In that way, I made it into college, but after happily reaching my final goal of cohabitation (with a local, beautiful, "bad" girl), I didn't know what I was supposed to aim for next. In reality, "shacking up" wasn't as wonderful as the manga made it out to be. ☺

It wasn't that college classes, clubs, or my part-time job was boring, but there just didn't seem to be that "spark"—I didn't seem to have passion. And in the end, my live-in, Hiroko, and I broke up.

In hindsight, I think I spent every day looking for that "something to be passionate about" when I was twenty. My emotions were in turmoil trying to figure out what I wanted to do with my life. Because I did not have confidence in myself, I meaninglessly compared myself to others around me.

"What do I want to do? What kind of work am I cut out for? I'll be in trouble if I continue like this. But what should I do?" I thought all alone to myself, knowing that I would not find the answers, regardless of how much thinking I did.

When I started to feel suffocated, I went out to karaoke houses with friends and totally screamed my lungs out to the songs of the Japanese indies punk rock band Blue Hearts in utter desperation. ☺ Every day seemed to be a desperate search for what I wanted to do with my life. I thought, "Surely, I, too, should be able to do something...."

STORY 1

MY BAR

- cocktails & dreams -

Twenty years old. Start up my own bar.

Yes, yes. It was around the time when I saw the movie *Cocktail* that I reached the biggest turning point of my life.

That was my day off as a part-time pizza delivery guy. In my small apartment, while eating my beef bowl bento, I watched the movie *Cocktail*, starring Tom Cruise. After watching the movie, I was seriously blown away!

Watching Tom Cruise make cocktails behind a lit up bar, spinning bottles and glasses, with rock music blaring in the background made me explode with excitement. "Wow! Too cool! I want to be a bartender and own a bar! Besides that, I'll be popular with the girls, and I'll be rich. What more could I want?" ☺ Well, if only someone would have said to me at that time, "This is just a movie. In the real world, it's not that easy to own a bar." But fortunately, my cat, Genki, was the only one nearby. ☺ So, I began running with the idea.

When I become interested in something, I have a habit of going to a bookstore. And that is exactly what I did then. I rushed to the local bookstore and bought everything from *How to Own a Shop,* to *A Guide to Opening Your Own Store,* to *Secrets to Business Prosperity,* and absorbed myself in reading.

As a result, I understood the hopeless reality that it would require tens of millions of yen to open a shop! For a moment, I thought, "Impossible. Goodbye dream...." But I was annoyed at the idea of giving up before even trying. I thought about it for a while. "Hmm. I don't want to just give up, but what should I do?" But thinking about it didn't start anything.

I changed my thinking to, "Well, I can figure out the money situation little by little. I'll try doing what I can do right now." For starters, I decided to train as a bartender while working part-time at a local bar.

When the time came for me to start work as a bartender, I discovered it was hard work. I was surprised. For the first month, all I did was wash dishes, clean, and worked as a go-fer for the senior bartenders. The reality gap was more intense for me because my image of a bartender was that of Tom Cruise in the movie. ☺

"I don't want to do this! This isn't cool at all! I should just quit!" I thought so many times, but quitting so soon would be lame, right? And I'd already declared to my friends and girlfriend that I'd try my best to start up my own bar. "Quitting because it was rough" would just be embarrassing in the first place. So, while enduring the treatment as scum, I seriously thought, "At this rate, as the dishwasher, it might take decades to have my own bar. What should I do in order to escape this life as dishwasher and become a real bartender?"

Well, the answer was simple. It all boiled down to ability. I was in the position of dishwasher because I made cocktails poorly, and what I needed to do was become better than the senior bartenders. "All right, I'll study cocktails on my own and beat the others!" I set that as my new goal and got fired up.

Starting immediately that day, I began the "twenty-one hours a day system" of pouring all of my time, except for three hours of sleep, into training as a bartender.

I bought a complete cocktail set for home, had my girlfriend play the customer, and started my thorough training. Truthfully, everything in life at that time was only about "becoming a bartender." The book *Bartender's Manual* was with me at all times. When I was watching TV, I was always spinning a bottle, and I even had cocktail recipes on a waterproof-type notebook for the bath.

My personal motto was "Hey! Ayumu! Are you working harder than Ichiro?" ☺

Naturally, you get results when you seriously absorb yourself in something you like.

Around three months into my training, the manager acknowledged me, and I was finally allowed to stand behind the counter as a full-fledged bartender. In doing so, I was seriously feeling the pleasures of bartending at last.

Every part of me began to yearn. "I do want to have a bar of my own after all!"

Since I started working as a bartender, I hadn't gone to classes at the college that I'd worked so hard to get in to. I had hardly made any friends, but there were three guys that I got along with: motorcycle-loving Kenta, hard-drinker Seiji, and flirty-musician Daisuke. ☺

In the beginning, I had thought to have my own bar, but gradually I started thinking, "If I could start a bar with these three, it would be so much fun."

I asked them, "Want to start a bar together?"

Well, it wasn't an immediate agreement of "Yeah! Let's do it!"

We all weren't that ignorant about the real world, but after watching *Cocktail* together, sharing drinks and passionate discussions it was, "All right! Let's do this, the four of us!"

We then began various preparations for starting up our bar. "First of all, we all need to train as bartenders!" we decided. We each worked in various restaurants and bars, getting together on our days off to brainstorm our bar name and image, and we went to bars to study menus.

Several months later, after all four of us gained some skills as bartenders, it was time to seriously start looking for a venue for our bar. We went to realtors in much the same manner as looking for an apartment and looked through real estate publications, but a cheap and geographically convenient space was not easy to find.

Just around that time, I heard that the bar I was working at was closing and would be renting out the space for six million yen.

At first, we were all excited. "Seriously? This is our chance! Let's make this our bar!"

But after we calmed down and thought about it, "Yeah. The bar is really cool but still six million is out of our reach." We settled on this all too common conclusion.

"We still don't have the skills anyways."

"The economy isn't good."

"We don't want to start this in debt anyway."

"It won't be too late after graduation."

Suddenly our hype dwindled down....

After the four of us decided, "It's hopeless. Let's give it up for now," I went home feeling really down. I was still thinking about it even after getting in to bed. I thought, "My life is always like this." It was that way when I was in elementary school and worked really hard at little league because I wanted to be a baseball player, and when I was in high school and seriously worked on the guitar because I wanted to be a guitarist. It was the same again when I was really passionate about becoming a professional surfer.

I realized that in the end, it was just a repeated pattern. When it came to that crucial moment, I'd get nervous, I'd run and hide, or I'd lose, and make convenient excuses for myself. What I was supposed to be "serious" about became "good as a hobby" and eventually faded out.

But this time we had worked so hard to get to where we were toward our dream to own a bar. When I realized that the same pattern of fading out might happen, my heart screamed out, "Hey! You gonna run away again?! No! This time, I'll try without running."

To be honest, I couldn't even begin to think how four penniless guys would get six million yen, and even if we could find the funds to start up a bar, what would we do if it failed and we ended up in debt hell and had wasted our lives. There were such worries, but feelings of "Now is the time to take a chance, or else my life will end with all defeats" started overflowing. I couldn't suppress it anymore.

I immediately discussed those feelings with the other three, and said, "Let's do this anyway!" Surprisingly, they all agreed. I guess it wasn't just me, but everyone had the same feelings after all. When we discovered that, we were all hyped up. In the end, the four of us excitedly agreed, "All right! Let's do this!" and began running with it again.

The next day was the beginning of our "fundraising hell days." We needed six million yen, so that was 1.5 million apiece. And the time limit specified by the realtor was one month! So, imagine being twenty years of age with one month to get 1.5 million yen. What in the world would you do?

The very first thing I did was to sell everything I owned. I sold everything: my guitar, motorcycle, stereo, books, CDs. The money I made from that was...a mere 180,000 yen! Oh well, over 1.3 million to go.

Next, I looked for high paying part-time work. At first, I went through the want ads over and over again but didn't find anything. Around this time, I heard a rumor, "You can make 50,000 yen for washing one corpse that's been soaked in formalin." At that, everyone jumped with excitement! "Yeah! 50,000 yen for one body, then thirty bodies and we're home free! I'll wash as many bodies as you want!" And with that excitement, we looked up university hospitals in the phonebook and started dialing one by one...but we were met with a cold-hearted reaction. "Body washing? Thirty bodies? Umm, it's not wartime now," we were told. ☺

I didn't find work after all.

In the same manner, I discovered high paying part-time work as a "human guinea pig." In other words, it's drug experimentation. With drugs, there are three phases in the experimentation process. The first phase is a rat. The second phase is a monkey. The third phase is "us"—healthy, young males. ☺ With an attitude of "well, we'll try anything" we applied, but...

On the day of the job, after showing up at the shady clinic, we were put on a bus like a scene out of *Battle Royale*. When we arrived at our destination, it was a hospital in the mountains of Ibaraki prefecture...once inside the hospital, they dressed us in white like some cult and stood us in a line. Then suddenly someone, a director, perhaps, handed me about ten pills and ordered, "You, swallow that!"

What I was testing was a drug that lowers blood pressure. I have pretty low blood pressure to begin with, so my memory goes blank after taking that drug. I fell asleep or fainted right away, and when I woke up I looked at the clock; sixteen hours had passed. This is seriously wrong. On top of that, my arm felt itchy and as I was rubbing my eyes from sleep, I notice there are dozens of marks and bruises from injections. It looked like track marks of a junkie. ☺ I immediately called for a nurse and asked, "What is this? Isn't this dangerous?"

The nurse answered, "Yes. We've taken blood hourly. This is regulation."

Thereafter, it was a parade of questioning, "Isn't this dangerous?" but somehow, I safely(?) completed the two night/three day human experiment.

Then at the end of it, they said, "Okay, you're done with the experiment, so you may smoke now." And so the six of us from the same group had a smoke while saying, "Ahh. So glad this experiment is all over." At that moment, five of the six fell to the ground. ☺ Of course, I also got dizzy and fell backwards from the chair the moment I inhaled. Our blood pressures were too low. Boy, was that a dangerous job. I wonder if that drug was really released. You never know what's working in the background in this world. Seriously scary. ☺

Well, after going through all that, I was only paid 80,000 yen. At this rate, I'd never get the 1.5 million, so out of desperation I asked the human experiment office, "Isn't there anything that I'd be able to make a lot of money at once?"

And they said, "Oh, yes there is."

"What? Really? What is it? What kind of job is it?" I asked filled with hope and fear.

Then the woman said, "It's a job that's known as 'crunch-crunch,' have you heard of it?"

How the hell would I know? ☺ So I asked, "What is that?" Basically, it's a job where they break your bones, 200,000 yen for an arm, and 600,000 yen for a leg!

We shouted, "600,000! No way!" ☺

Apparently, this experiment's purpose was to research the mechanism of bones breaking in athletes, and they needed to take x-rays of the process while a vise-like machine slowly breaks the bone...this job is seriously crazy. The woman proudly added, "All medical and hospital costs that occur after the bone is broken will be covered entirely."

We all barked back, "They sure better be!" ☺

Well, starting up the bar with all four employees having broken legs wouldn't get us anywhere. We did joke, however, that "it'd be kind of cool, a 'flamingo bar' with all employees one-legged!" ☺ But still, there was an atmosphere of "no way!"

Even with the four of us individually raising funds for a 1.5 million yen goal, everyone can't raise funds in the exact same way. A comparatively sociable type like me is okay, but of the four of us, Kenta is a bit of the shy type. He wasn't getting anywhere. So naturally, there developed an unspoken feeling among us of "all of us would be impossible, but Kenta should at least do the 'crunch-crunch' experiment." ☺ And yeah, I was the one creating that atmosphere. Kenta picked up on this and said, "I'll go." The three of us, the ones that pressured him, say "Seriously?" with a straight face. We're terrible.

Kenta's decision was meaningless in the end. He didn't pass the physical exam and wasn't able to participate in the 'crunch-crunch' experiment. ☺ Oops.

Well, well. After this and that, I'd sold all of my belongings for 180,000 yen, made 80,000 yen as a human guinea pig, bringing the grand total to 260,000 yen. Almost two weeks had already passed. "1,240,000 yen remaining in 2 more weeks! Yikes!" I was starting to get really nervous.

What I did next was the "hit up friends, acquaintances, and everyone I know strategy." With yearbooks and address books in hand, I called everyone I'd ever spoken to in my life. It would start out from "Long time. How've you been?" and then I would somehow bring the conversation to "Could you lend me some money?" I think everyone feels this way, but I hate borrowing money from friends. The more phone calls I made, the more I felt like I was digging myself deeper into a hole.

"I haven't heard from you in a year and a half, and all of a sudden you're asking for money?"
"Running a successful bar isn't that easy. That's just too big of a gamble."
"Is this some kind of cult?"
"A pyramid scheme?"
"Are you okay? You sure you're not being played?"
Most of my friends declined with this kind of negativity. I was filled with worry that I'd lose all of my friends if I kept this up.

Only those friends who I saw regularly supported the idea. "That sounds great! Good luck!" many of them said. But the fact that we regularly hung out together meant that we had the same financial status—poor. Nobody had any spare money to lend. I wanted to yell, "Not encouragement, but cash!" ☺ Well, since I was twenty at the time, it's a given that everyone my age wouldn't have any money.

But there were also really incredible friends.
"Ayumu, if you're serious about this, I'll support you. Take it." a hoodlum friend lent me 100,000 yen, no questions asked. Another friend lent me several hundreds of thousands of yen and said, "I've been saving up, so please use this. I believe in you, Ayumu."

Or the childhood friend who went into debt to lend me money.

And just like that, the funds started to add up by repeating such thankful and encouraging scenes. I was almost in tears just to think that I had people who would go to such lengths for me, even though I could not guarantee anything.

In the end, when the one month was up...the four of us were able to come up with 6.2 million yen! "We did it! Yes! Ha!" the four of us drank and danced and celebrated at Daisuke and Kenta's apartment. "Wow! It's our bar! Yay! Yay!" ☺

The very next day, we paid the realtor and formally signed the contract, and freely began preparations for opening up our bar. Every night after that, we stayed at the bar overnight fighting over this and that, creating our bar. Inside the bar where cool neon signs flickered, our favorite rock music echoed loudly. It felt like a school festival and it was really a lot of fun.

Then, the winter of my twenty-first year, our bar, "Rockwell's," opened.

Various friends, from childhood to university, showed up and the opening party was in full swing. After the party was over and everyone had left, when it was barely daylight, and after we had cleaned up, the four of us toasted, "Good job! It is finally here!" I was so incredibly happy at that moment. A good kind of fatigue and a crazily huge emotion seeped throughout my entire body.

At that moment, I saw in front of me the scene I had envisioned all that time. The exact scene, the four of us toasting on opening night, that I had envisioned to help pick myself up when things didn't go well and I became discouraged, was there in front of me. "Is this déjà vu?" I thought. It was exactly the way I had envisioned it—where the four of us were situated, the lighting, and even the brand of beer we each had in hand—that it really gave me goose bumps. I enjoyed that moment, for that scene was what we had worked so hard to achieve. It was truly a great night.

Although we happily started up the bar, reality wasn't that easy. ☺ When we first opened, various friends would come to the bar and things were good, but after about a month, there was nobody. Since we started the place with mostly loans, we felt a real sense of impending crisis seeing the deserted and lonely bar.

At such times, humans are weak. Once the popularity wore off, we gradually started losing confidence in ourselves. We originally began this with feelings of "Let's make this into a place that says we're great, regardless of what anyone says!" But that turned into "slow business; can't make loan payments; serious trouble; will do anything for business to pick up" and before we knew it, we had killed our feelings, recklessly incorporated trends, copied other bars that were getting better business, and were going in every different direction with each customer's opinions. And in doing so, we lost customers and sales decreased. It was really a vicious cycle.

I think it was about six months after we opened the bar. The four of us sat down one night after closing and had a serious discussion. Since we had started this, there was hardly a salary and we faced the reality that we would go out of business if things kept up this way; the four of us looked pale. ☺

Well, while we were having a truthful talk there for the first time in a long while, we got over it and our depressing feelings brighten up. "We originally weren't the type of guys to adopt trends, right? So let's go back to our original plan again. Just as we had wanted to in the beginning, let's make this into a bar that the four of us think is great! If that is something that customers don't take to, then we can give up with no regrets, close up shop, and we can all go work at a delivery company. If the four of us worked for a year, we should be able to pay off the entire loan."

We agreed, "Yeah. Let's try what we feel is 'right' and if that doesn't work, we'll be able to accept it."

"All right. We have to do this!"

"Yeah!" we exploded together.

From that point on, in a sense, it was a destruction process. ☺All of the common knowledge rules about "how to prosper" were broken, and we plunged into a "100 percent self-satisfaction mode" that involved only what we felt was "right." We stocked the bar completely with only the liquor we liked. We only played music we liked in the bar. We collected our favorite things and redecorated the interior as if it were our bedrooms. If a rude customer came in, we ran the place in an unflattering style saying, "We didn't start this place to serve drinks to people like you. So leave."

At first, as we changed our style of running the bar to better suit us, we lost more customers…

"That's just for your own satisfaction."

"You don't understand what business is."

"You don't know the first thing about customer service."

"The customer needs are this and that…"

But I think it was about that time that "our bar" in the real sense began. More and more people that we thought of as "cool" became regulars, there were more ardent fans who would tell us "This is a great bar!", and slowly but surely the business was taking off. That flow steadily accelerated. We could feel the change in the atmosphere. I started to really enjoy working there, and as if in return, sales continued to rise. We truly realized the importance of continuing to believe in ourselves.

Through those up and downs, our bar became a big hit. From that point on, it came all at once! As a result, with new friends who shared our spirit joining us, Rockwell's branched out to four establishments in two years.

GREAT!!

With multiple bars, we had more friends. We created a club called "Heaven" with the employees and the customers. That club was fun, too!

We held events we called "Sorry If You Die! Tours" starting with "Bungee Jumping Tournament without a Bungee" which was nothing but diving off a twenty meter high bridge at a local lake. We tried the "Snowy Mountain Disaster Tour!" that entailed nothing but climbing snowcapped mountains and causing frostbite for many, and we even attempted an all-night twelve-hour cornering competition bike race.

To think of it now, it is a wonder that no one did die through such dangerous tours. ☺

Another fun thing that happened was the "Let's Try and Meet Sathya Sai Baba Tour," which came about when a discussion about whether or not he was real escalated into, "Screw it! Let's just go and find out!" and we went all the way to India. By coincidence, I was chosen out of the 5,000 people at Sathya Sai Baba's temple to go to the interview room and had a personal interview with him. He was real, after all! ☺

Influenced by Mother Teresa, we also held a different type of event called "The 500 Santa Clauses." We gathered 500 presents, mostly with our customers' help, and participated in Christmas parties and passed out presents at various orphanages and homes for children with disabilities. That too, was a wonderful experience. Hooked on Jacques Mayol's *Homo Delphinus: The Dolphin within Man*, we all went swimming with dolphins, too.

Well, it was a group of people who basically had to immediately try something if they thought "That sounds like fun!" so decisions were made promptly. Nobody would listen to things like "There's no time" or "I don't have any money."

"Okay, whatever. But are you going or not?"

"Yeah, I'll go."

It was simple like that and it felt good.

In those days, everything went smoothly. We had four bars, and an abundance of great friends. Various media had put us in the spotlight, and we were making some money. Those days were so much fun, because in a sense, we had worked so hard up until then, aiming for that situation.

But...
To be frank, as a sense of "we're on track" drifted within us, the fun in the true sense or the anticipation began to fade within me. I began to feel like "What am I supposed to aim for now?" I could have forced a new goal like "hundreds of millions of yen a year!" or "let's go for one hundred bars next!"...but for some reason, that didn't excite me.

So, I asked myself once again slowly, "What now? Where to?"

Then my heart screamed, "You can't cling to small successes forever! Go back to being nothing and start over from zero. Challenge and refine yourself!"

At that moment, I felt strangely refreshed. I decided to immediately quit the bar and return to being nothing.

However, I had made it this far because my friends and I had done it all together. At first I thought, "After making it this far, how could I—the leader—quit now?" But the desire to leave didn't die down; instead it was growing. At last, it came to the point where I had no choice but to tell my friends who worked at the bar with me.

When I gave up and spoke honestly, they all understood. We understood each other at the fundamental level. "If you feel that way, Ayumu, it can't be helped," they said and accepted it warmly.

On the last night, all of my friends, who worked so hard for our bar, and I went to a karaoke house, and yet again, we were screaming Blue Hearts' songs. We sang the song "The Song that Never Ends" over and over again. That scene remains in my heart.

And I officially left the bar. I went back to being nothing with no management rights or anything, of course.

I was twenty-three years old.

MY BOOK

~ Keep sanctuary in your heart ~
Twenty-three years old.
Start our own publishing company.

From the day I returned to being nothing, I had an incredible amount of time and an incredible amount of freedom. I didn't have any money at all, but I didn't have anything I needed to do, either. I said, "Okay, 360 degrees. I can go in any direction and do anything!"

Because I originally had no intentions to use my past successful experience in restaurant management to take it to the next level, I spent my days as just another guy with nothing, as if reborn with a clean slate.

"What do I want to do next? I guess I can work part-time with a moving company while I try to figure it out." And for a while, I hung out, played pachinko, and barhopped. On the afternoons when I was really bored, I went to the park to play with the local kids. ☺

During that time, I went to the bookstore with Masaki. The two of us were talking in front of the autobiography section, and the conversation led to "Wouldn't it be cool if my autobiography was here? Marie Curie, Hideyo Noguchi, Ayumu Takahashi, Einstein...." Our conversation escalated to, "Wouldn't it be so cool that a twenty-three-year-old guy who isn't even famous—who just bought the Japanese pop group Dreams Come True CD at Tower Records—came out with his autobiography?" We joked, "Instead of writing an autobiography because you are a great person, write an autobiography and become a great person. Yeah? Wanna?" But the joking gradually became a serious discussion. "Yeah. Umm, so, what do we need to do in order to sell an autobiography?" We had gone into reality mode before we knew it. ☺

That is how the "Autobiography Project" came about with Masaki and me. Well, in the process of reading books and researching, we slowly realized that in order to sell your own book, you needed to submit a proposal to a publishing company and have them approve it. But we began saying, "That seems like way too much work. Why do we need someone else's approval for our own book?" As a result, in the end we decided, "Screw it. We'll just start our own publishing company!" If I think about it now, this was the beginning of the test. ☺

Not knowing the first thing about publishing, we were completely hyped. Right away, we started recruiting friends to create a passionate publishing company! In addition to Masaki and myself, my little brother, Minoru (a boy who loved American football and dolphins) and Kon (a guy who raced a converted Skyline on the Tokyo Bay Highway) joined us. That is how the publishing company, with four members with an average age of twenty, came into existence. The company name was easily and quickly decided on—Sanctuary Publishing—taking the name from our favorite manga, "Sanctuary."

We had no clue as to how much money we needed in order to start a publishing company. So, illogically, we said, "Like the bar, let's just get six million yen!" and yet again dived right into those fundraising hell days. Basically, we did our usual "sell everything, human guinea pig, call everyone in the yearbook..."! ☺ But this time around, it went comparatively smoother than before—perhaps we had built up immunity?—and we gathered six million yen.

It was great that we had raised the funds, but we were a publishing company that knew nothing about publishing. We said we were a publishing company, but we didn't know what we were fundamentally supposed to be doing. ☺ First, we researched how to make a book, and we finally determined that they are made at printing companies. After one week, we had finally reached the point of "So, what printing company are we going to use?" I told everyone, in my usual completely confident manner with absolutely no basis, "We're going to make a bestseller, so a small, local printing company won't do. We need to do business with one of the top ten in Japan!" and the ordeal began. ☺

Immediately, the four of us split up to go around to the top ten printing companies. We had put on our brand new suits, but nine out of the ten companies turned us away at the front desk. But the chief of sales at the one remaining company said, "You guys will succeed! I'll support you!" I was truly happy. On top of that, this guy taught us step by step the basics of publishing. And due to that, our company quickly became more like a publishing company.

I then desperately began writing my autobiography, making full use of my elementary school level writing skills. Everyone else went around to the bookstores throughout the country as sales representatives to have our book sold in their stores. "We don't know the rules of the publishing industry, but let's completely exhaust whatever we feel is the right way for us!" we decided, and we all did whatever we could for that first autobiography to sell.

Finally, it was the day the book went on the market! When I saw the memorial first book for our Sanctuary Publishing Company, my autobiography *Heaven's Door* stacked on the shelves at the Shinjuku Isetan Bookstore, I was really moved. "Yes! For sure, a bestseller! Publishing is easy!" the four of us agreed and celebrated.

But, as always, it wasn't that easy. ☺ My first autobiography hardy sold at all. "Seriously? Why?" I was so shocked. Thinking back, I have no idea why an amateur group had so much confidence, but we believed that the book would sell. And when it didn't sell at all, we were flabbergasted.

For a while, the four of us were at a loss. But this was only our first book, so we figured "Things like this happen. Let's move on! Next!" With the addition of new members, we changed our outlook and cheerfully moved forward.

But we did not readily get any results. When our second book, a collection of essays on dolphins written by my brother, Minoru, and our third book, a novel written by a friend, were published and did not sell at all, a serious sense of "If this keeps up, we're in deep trouble. Our company will go bankrupt..." drifted among us.

The initial six million yen was long gone with new debt to make loan payments on. Our company was barely maintaining. There was no salary, of course. And there was one problem after another. No new books were completed...we were in the worst state. I couldn't blame them in that state, but because of it, the others quit one by one, and in the end, it was me, my brother, Minoru, and a three million yen debt.

At that point, I was depressed, as would be expected. This time the amount of debt wasn't at a level that we could quit and work at a delivery company to pay it off. ☺ "If we don't give up and work toward creating something that we believe is great, the results will surely follow," is my philosophy. But at that time, even my belief was shaken.

But hey, being depressed wasn't going to sell books. We had to do whatever we could do in that moment. I desperately told myself "Only look forward from where you are." Out of desperation, I tried to pick myself up while I drank: "Worrying about this and that won't do you any good. Move on! Next book! Think only about the next book. That is all you need to do! You can do this! Another beer please!" ☺

The fourth book we took a chance on was titled *Begin by Quitting*. We published the book filled with feelings of "be true to yourself in life." That became our very first hit! Yay!

Since this was our first book that sold, we only realized this when we saw the piles of letters from readers and order forms from bookstores around the country. We were really impressed. I was happy. Because, during that time, we had worked so hard, spending all night, every night at the office, it felt like we were being rewarded for our efforts, which made me even happier.

While reading the letters that arrived from readers, it was the first time ever that I sensed "even guys like us can be a support to so many lives through this thing called a book." I felt from the very core of my being the rewards of publishing for the first time. From the bottom of my heart, I was glad that we had started a publishing company after all. And for me, that got me excited! ☺

After that, we published a collection of wise words from the people we respected, my second autobiography, the greatest guidebook on how to start your own shop or publish your own book, and an inspirational book of the passionate professional wrestler, Antonio Inoki. And almost all of the books were a hit!

While new members joined us and published many hits, we created the books we wanted to create; our very pleasurable Sanctuary Publishing had burst onto the path of success.

It seemed more like a band than a company. Always working together, drinking together, traveling together...the individual color of each of the members melted together perfectly. With those friends, those days were spent thoroughly enjoying the pleasures of creating a book and conveying the message to many people. Although, as always, we didn't get enough sleep. ☺

Then came the summer I turned twenty-six. The time had come for this publishing project to finally end.

We had made a promise to each other when the going was the roughest—"Let's give it our all for two years. Until then, let's become overwhelmed and then go our separate ways with pride." That time had arrived. To me, it seemed the publishing company was getting on track; therefore, I had an overflowing desire to return once again to being nothing and challenging myself to do something new from scratch.

On the night we all discussed going our separate ways, my friend Tsuru, who had worked hard with us through it all, said, "I want to stay in publishing forever, so I'll take on Sanctuary Publishing." Thanks to him, even now after more than twelve years since I'd left, Sanctuary Publishing is still a hard-core energetic publisher that continues to grow.

The last night, August 30, 1998, was the best night. At Tokyo's Odaiba beach, we made ourselves a ONE NIGHT BAR and brought tons of champagne (Dom Perignon!), beer, sushi, and pizza. After we all had champagne and beer fights, we made a toast! Just as everyone was a bit tipsy, I suggested "the first and last serious talk" where each person says a few words to the other members. Though it was a bit embarrassing to say serious words of gratitude to those friends who we usually see daily, it was a time for everyone to express and exchange the greatest feelings in their respective ways. Looking at my friends' faces, those who were there from the beginning struggles up until the very last night, gave me flashbacks to various scenes. We were all grown adults, but cried like children. And, well, of course, I cried like a baby too. ☺

At the end of the night, we all sang the song "Sora" that we had written together, dove into the water, and said our farewells to the journey we called Sanctuary.

Keep sanctuary in your heart.

Ayumu Takahashi.
Twenty-six years old.
Summer.
Yet again, back to being a cheerful nothing.
Okay, what's next?

STORY 3

WORLD JOURNEY

~ LOVE & FREE ~
**A journey to roam the world
with my wife at twenty-six**

After returning to nothing, I married Sayaka, my girlfriend of six years, and traveled the world!

What started it was, again, quite simple.

"Hey, Sayaka. If you had all seven dragon balls and could wish for anything, what would you do?"

"Hmm. Well, if I had only one wish, I guess I'd want to go around the world with you."

"Wow! Around the world? That sounds great!"

It all began like that, with a couple's typical conversation in a Shinjyuku café. ☺

But seriously though, up until then I had done various things with my friends. Then I decided to get married and then would be free to do anything I liked with Sayaka. The instant I heard the words "around the world," a switch turned on in my head.

"All right! Around the world! Let's really do it!" I declared, but then thought, "How much would that cost anyway?" As usual, I went straight to the bookstore, looked through various books, and came up with nothing. ☺

It's common sense, but every guidebook pointed out that the cost could vary depending on different routes, time, accommodations, and transportation. And there was an infinite amount of information on interesting countries that made it just about impossible to decide on a route.

I cut to the chase and said, "Ah, I hate this! It's too much of a hassle. Let's just save as much money as we can and leave three days after the wedding! No route mapped out. No time frame. Let's just look at a map of the world and go whichever way our hearts desire. And, well, we can return when we run out of money."

I immediately started working to save up money for our journey.

I left Sanctuary Publishing with practically nothing, so I was starting from zero. We only had about two months until we were to leave, so I began working the next day, doing anything I could. I worked part time at a moving company, did some day labor construction work, did a few talk shows, saved the money that people gave to us as a wedding gift, got some credit cards and took out cash advances (oh, I guess that wouldn't really be saving?). I had been president of a company recently. What was I doing? ☺

Somehow, I saved up some money doing various things, and we flew out from Narita Airport three days after the wedding, headed toward Australia. Sayaka's desire was to go first to the Great Barrier Reef.

It was a year and eight months of traveling together in any which way our hearts desired. With huge packs on our backs, a small traveler's guitar and harmonica in hand, we wandered the world through dozens of countries from the North Pole to the South Pole.

Let me give you a rough outline of our journey.

First, we started from Cairns on the continent of Australia and worked our way clockwise. We slowly made our way around the continent using long distance buses and rental cars. We also stopped off at the South Pole, which was a wonderful world of blue and white.

Then, from Bali in Indonesia, we traveled to Singapore, the Philippines, Malaysia, and Thailand. From the route through Southeast Asia, we entered India and went to Mother Teresa's institutions and the Ganges River. Next, we took a bus to Nepal to get a taste of the Himalayas.

From there we went north, and after staying with a nomadic family in Mongolia, we moved on to the Siberian Railroad. We arrived in Moscow after crossing Eurasia, stopping off at Lake Baikal. After taking our time to enjoy Moscow, we went to Finland, and went even further north to the Arctic Circle.

Next, we traveled through European countries, starting from the United Kingdom. We traveled through The Netherlands, France, and then further south through Spain. From the southernmost point of Spain, we crossed the Strait of Gibraltar into Morocco, the northernmost point of the African continent, and then to the Sahara Desert and the oases I had longed to see. After traveling to the Middle Eastern countries of Egypt and Israel, we returned to the continent of Africa and thoroughly enjoyed the wild kingdom in Kenya. Then it was time for the beach! We spent time relaxing at the island of Mauritius, famous for having the world's best beaches.

We then flew directly to Peru in South America. After seeing Machu Picchu, the Nazca Lines, and several other world heritage sites, we flew to Chile's Easter Island to meet the Moai statues. From there, we took a relaxing island trip to Tahiti, then went north in the Pacific to Hawaii. After that, we flew to Los Angeles and traveled north, until we reached our goal, Alaska! That's how the journey went.

In one word, it was simply fun. Although people often ask, "What country was the most interesting? Where would you recommend?" there's no way I can answer! ☺ I can say that India, Mongolia, the Sahara Desert, Kenya, and Alaska left the strongest impressions on me.

But everybody has different tastes and I'm sure that timing plays a role, so my thoughts probably are not much help, right? ☺ I do think that the key to this particular journey was that I made it with my wife, Sayaka.

Before we were married, Sayaka was an office worker in Ginza, not quite the "hungry and wild" type, but rather more of a "Chanel and Prada" type person. And here I am compared to that. ☺ We are completely different in every aspect, from the things we want to do, the things we want to see, the things we like, our sense of money, physical strength, thought processes, to our sense of values.

Therefore, it was a great adventure in itself to undetake this journey together. We literally quarreled almost every day. With the exception of a particularly safe country, we spent almost all of our time together excluding shower and toilet time, with no place to run. As a result, we had to face each other's complaints or differences, discuss them, and work them out one by one. Regardless of the fact that she is my wife, it was the first time I had ever deeply faced another person.

But I realize now how valuable that time was. I knew how to live happily for myself, but it's different to live happily together. It would be cool to say "intuition connects us" but I realized that in order to maintain happiness for the both of us, it takes an enormous amount of communication and time spent together. At least this is how it was for us.

For two to be one. For two to be two.

I spent those days with that thought...and I am still desperately struggling! ☺

Another key to our journey is that all of the encounters we had with others made a big impact on me. I know that it's very ordinary, but I strongly feel it did.

During the journey, I was impressed over and over again by experiencing the various lifestyles on earth, encountering various people, and thinking "this can be a way of life too" or "that way of life is nice too." Before the journey, I thought I understood "a way of life for each." But through this journey, I experienced even more values, various forms of happiness, and ways of life. I feel that my lifestyle choices or my freedom of lifestyles have greatly expanded.

It was because I met so many absolutely wonderful people who weren't all in to titles or achievements or age. I think that feeling of "people are interesting because they are so different" was strongly renewed within me.

Let me take this opportunity to introduce the beautiful people I met on my journey around the world and around Japan.

Getting to know others is getting to know oneself.

Well, relax and enjoy.

Encounters on the Streets of the World

People #1: Holland

"I just simply love hammocks. It's not about how good it feels to sleep in, but I just love the actual existence of them. So I've collected hammocks from around the world, working locally to fund my travels for more than six years. And last year, I was finally able to open this shop."

These are the words of a Dutch woman who runs a hammock shop in Amsterdam. Her shop was packed with over a hundred different kinds of hammocks. She was wonderful.

People #2: USA

"Cats, cats, cats, from sun up to sun down. I've lost sleep because of cats. I've run out of money because of cats. I can't travel because of cats. But if I see a cat in need, I can't just leave it. Even if I have complaints, I just have to. It's like I live for cats."

These are the words of a middle-aged American woman who runs a rescue organization for strays in New York City. She spends most days going out after work finding a new home for the stray cats she picks up before the pound "disposes" of them.

People #3: Australia

"I enjoy exchanging our lives with the strangers I meet, like this. I go wherever I want, whenever I want, freely, in whatever direction my heart desires. I've lived this way for over twenty years. Not having any money won't kill me."

These are the words of a hippie named David, living on the beach of Byron Bay, Australia. Walking the beaches, playing a strange flute, he would approach tourists and strike up a conversation.

People #4: Australia

I love the lyrics "world with no borders" in the song *Imagine* by John Lennon. But I can't play the guitar or sing, so this small store called *ONE WORLD* is my way of expressing that."

These are the words of a man who runs a small variety store in a small town in Australia. In the corner of the store, lined with trinkets from around the world, sat a simple sign with the store's name *ONE WORLD*, but it overflowed with hand-made warmth.

People #5: Australia

"Weekends are for spending time with your family in nature. That is when I can really go back to being my true self."

These are the words of a father happily cooking with his children at a campground in Australia. I encountered many such fathers, because in Australia, not only are businesses closed, but also department stores are closed on the weekends.

People #6: India

"There is nothing happier than to die right here."

These are the words of an elderly man bathing in the Ganges River, India. In order to die in this place, he left his family whom he had spent dozens of years with, to live on the banks of the river in a shack as a beggar awaiting, "the day the body becomes ashes and returns to the Ganges River."

People #7: Indonesia

"I sing for her; I live for her. I'll sing with all of that happiness and sorrow. I don't want to be famous, nor do I want money. I may not even really enjoy playing the guitar. I am just trying my best to make her happy."

These are the words of a young Indonesian singing with a guitar in hand on the streets of Ubud on the island of Bali. He, who says "she is everything to me" lives to sing for her, working part-time twice a week to cover living expenses.

People #8: Peru

"When I was younger, I just wanted money. That was everything. But now, I am happy to be living together with my family in this country."

These are the words of a Peruvian man who had just returned to his country after spending time in Japan as a migrant worker. He spoke to me in Cusco, the world's closest city to the sky.

People #9: Australia

"Love and peace."

These are the words of an American "junk artist" who has traveled for years and continues to gain fans around the world. When he arrives in a country, he goes to the junk yard to collect odds and ends, uses the junk to create art pieces, sells the pieces on the street, and when he's made enough money, he moves on to the next country. On top of that, he continues to donate a portion of his sales to the underprivileged children of that country. This was his response when asked, "What thoughts go into your work?"

People #10: Russia

"I'm happy if I can help the Russian and the Japanese to become friends. It's not just limited to Russians and Japanese, but I think that countries fight each other because they don't know much about each other. Therefore, I want to live my life in order to give Russians and Japanese a chance to get to know one another."

These are the words of a Russian female college student studying Japanese who I met in a car on the Trans-Siberian Railway. While studying world history, she became interested in the beautiful spirit of the Japanese people, and as a summer job, she was traveling with a group of Japanese tourists in another car as their tour guide.

People #11: England

"Because I clean, it makes everyone feel good. I don't know what others would say, but I am proud. I'm happy to be able to do this job."

These are the words of a beautiful blonde woman cheerfully working in a dark subway restroom, in London. In response to my saying, "This must be a tough job," because I felt there was such a gap between her youth and beautiful looks and the toilet cleaning.

People #12: the Philippines

"Life in the city with an abundance of high technology is nice, but simple technology and the ocean are all I need to feel great every day. I love this ocean, and I just want to protect it. That's all."

These are the words of youths protecting the ocean, living in a fishing village on the Sulu Sea of the Philippines. While other youths their age left for the cities, these guys said, "We want to be with the ocean we love till death."

People #13: Spain

"I sailed around the world for twenty years because I hated doing the same thing every day. But I changed on the day I found the woman I love. Now, every day is spent making two round trips on this Strait of Gibraltar, in order to have a life with the wife and children I love. But I swear to God, I am the happiest I have ever been. My adventure ended when I found my treasure, my wife."

These are the words of a sailor I met on the deck of the ship crossing the Strait of Gibraltar from the southernmost point of Spain to Morocco on the African continent.

People #14: Mongolia

"For my family to safely survive. That, in and of itself, is my happiness."

These are the words of an elderly nomadic man in the Gobi Desert of Mongolia. In a place only a few hours by plane from Tokyo, there are people who live as nomads on barren land without enough food, water, hospitals, or medicine.

People #15: Morocco

"We don't play music for money. Music is necessary to feel the happiness of right now, in this very moment."

These are the words of young nomads I met in the Sahara Desert. They drummed away on beautiful percussion instruments I had never seen before, just for the two of us. This was in response to my easygoing comment of "That's awesome! If you're this good, you should debut and make some serious money!"

People #16: Tibet

"Quit traveling and go back to your own country. To live where you were born is the best form of happiness."

I met a woman at a Tibetan refugee camp at the foot of the Himalayas. She was forced by the Chinese army from her own country and had just spent two months with her two children crossing over the Himalayas. The sign that read "FREE TIBET" stung at that moment. With a bit of sadness in her eyes, these were her parting words to me.

People #17: India

"I live my life with a theme each year. This year's theme is "festivals of the world" so our days are one festival after another after another. I like this kind of extreme lifestyle."

These are the words of a young Japanese guy I met at the Calcutta airport in India. He has spent the last five years working his butt off for three months, then spends what he makes on the remaining nine months to travel the world on whatever theme he had decided. His theme for last year, by the way, was "drink and party with the world" and he said he drank with people from more than fifty different countries. ☺ Nice!

People #18: India

"When I am drawing, I feel like I can surpass the limits of time. In my heart, I can travel in time to India 3,000 years ago. That feeling is supreme bliss."

These are the words of a wandering Japanese artist I met in Calcutta, India. He has been wandering the world for thirty years to draw, and then returns to Japan to open an exhibition.

People #19: the Philippines

"It's heaven here. I left my family in Japan and came here two years ago, but every day is filled with happiness. This is freedom here, isn't it?"

These are the words of a Japanese man living in Manila, the capital of the Philippines.

People #20: Japan

"I love sunsets more than my three daily meals, more than my wife."

These are the words of a man who continues to chase sunsets all over Japan and at last is able to make a living as a "sunset critic."

People #21: Japan

"At any rate, sex."

These are the words of a marvelous "sex lady" who takes pride in that fact that she has slept with nearly 1,000 men. She says she loves sex and to sleep with men is her reason to live.

People #22: Japan

"Here, food and lodging expenses are cheap. I work two or three times a week whenever I feel like it. And there's nobody that tells you what to do. This here is the best life."

These are the words of a man living and working day labor construction in Sanya, Tokyo, otherwise known as the "slums of Japan."

People #23: Japan

"Though my life is nowhere near fabulous, attending a public high school, attending a national university, and working as a public employee, I am the type that finds stable daily life appealing, which may be unusual. So, I'm very satisfied with my life right now."

These are the words of a man, who works for the postal service, who I met at a bar in Chiba Prefecture.

People #24: Japan

"My dream is to become Miki Imai's woman."

These are the words of a man, while working in a pub in Tokyo's gay district of Shinjuku's 2-chome, making every effort to be a woman like Miki Imai. Apparently, a poster of Miki Imai is properly hung inside the pub. ☺

People #25: Japan

"I've dyed cloth in rivers around the world, but Sumida River is it. My everything lies here. I hope to live my life with this river."

These are the words of an Edo Yuzen craftsman who had continued to stick to Sumida River.

People #26: Japan

"There are a lot of things, but protecting my family is what's important in life. That's all."

These are the words of an agricultural man in Yonezawa-shi, Yamagata Prefecture.

People #27: Japan

"Cooking, laundry, cleaning, child care...even the job of a housewife or housework is very deep. My goal at the moment is to master the role of housewife. In doing so, if everyone in the family is pleased, that would make me happy."

These are the words of my friend T's mother, a really beautiful and always cheerful woman. In response to my question, "I don't mean to be rude, but isn't it a bit boring to always be at home?"

People #28: Japan

"I'm not interested in whether it becomes a reality. Because fantasizing is what I live for."

These are the words of an unusual unemployed man in his fifties, who has never had to work due to the huge inheritance left by his parents. Others in the area called him the "delusional old man."

People #29: Japan

"I don't care what kind of job I have. I'm not trying to express myself through work. It's fine as long as I make enough to live, working properly without causing any trouble for coworkers. Anyway, it's all about motorcycles."

These are the words of my friend N who loves motorcycles and says he's happy as long as he's riding. He is consistent in that, while graduating from a top university, he chose to work for a small low-paying company for the sole reason that it was located near the motorcycle course.

People #30: Japan

"I'm here at this institution because it makes me happy to feel that I am useful to someone else. I work here because I can feel happiness. I've had people say, 'Quit playing the part of a good person.' But this job isn't easy enough to do just for the opinions of others. In short, I work for myself."

These are the words of my friend K who works in an institution for people with disabilities. Surely he is running around that institution with his big voice again today.

People #31: Japan

"If my children can live a fun and happy life, even if it is ordinary, I have no other expectations."

My mother, who lives in Yokohama, had a habit of saying this. ☺

At this very moment, there are six billion people on earth, and there are six billion different ways of life, different values, and different forms of happiness.
There truly are various ways of living.

Through everyday life, we tend to think inside a small box, but being born on such a planet, I feel that I want to see, touch, and feel various things to freely choose a life for myself.

What I know right now is merely the tip of the iceberg. Earth is huge! Life is short!

While I strongly felt "I'll see more and more of everything! I'll eat everything! I'll meet people! I'll feel! I'll play!"...

First, I guess I have to start saving. ☺
Okay, I'm going to work cheerfully again today! ☺

And right after I had turned twenty-eight, we finished our trip around the world and returned to Japan.

The first thing I discussed with Sayaka then was...

"Hey, it's good to be back and all, but where are we going to live?"

STORY 4

ISLAND PROJECT

~ ocean & sky ~

Twenty-eight years old. Return to home country.
The Island Project begins
on a remote island of Okinawa.

After returning to Japan from our journey around the world, Sayaka and I slowly traveled around Japan in search of a place to live.

During that trip we had an intense encounter with Okinawa. Originally, I was extremely conscious of the land called Okinawa since reading Kenjiro Haitani's *Child of the Sun* back in my teenage days. For the first time, I was able to enjoy every bit of it on this trip.

Then, I was blown away. I fell in love. To name the wonders of Okinawa in detail would be endless, but just as when one falls in love with a person, I don't really know why. It just felt great! Sayaka and I had been traveling around Okinawa on a motorcycle, and suddenly we were at a realtor's office deciding on a place to live. ☺ Okinawa truly has an enormous power. ☺

Well, it was nice moving to Okinawa, but the husband needed to hurry up and start working. ☺ We wouldn't be able to support ourselves without work.

I had continued to think about what I wanted to do next, but there was one idea I had during the journey that I thought might be it. It was...to create the best paradise, surrounded by nature on some island, with congenial friends. The idea came to me when I saw Coco Loco Island in the Philippines. It was an island that seemed like an adult version of a school festival, with a group of people who got along noisily but were self-sufficient in everything. While I joined in that atmosphere and did various things with them, I sparked. "This is fun! This feels good! I want to have an island with friends, too!" ☺ Well, I figured since I was Japanese, it would be best on an island in Japan. And it had to have beautiful beaches. I went from those thoughts to my encounter with Okinawa. Bingo! ☺ I shouted out, "Island Project: a strategy to create a paradise on a remote island of Okinawa!" and before I knew it, I had started a new project.

Although I had said "a paradise on a remote island of Okinawa," I had no idea exactly where to begin. And well, worrying about it wouldn't get me anywhere, so I decided first to start a "hideout" in Yomitanson on the main island of Okinawa. The hideout would be a shop where interesting people from around the world could come together and stay, drink, and hold events. I thought that the hideout could serve as base camp for the Island Project.

At first, I wandered around Okinawa looking for property, walking along the beach warehouse district, and visiting local real estate agents, but I didn't find anything that appealed to me. But, the God of Okinawa was kind. ☺ One day, I accidentally happened upon a villa with a private beach! It was perfect. I had decided instantly, "I've found it! This is it!"

So, with the help of a friendly realtor, I found the owner of the property and called to plead, "Please let us rent the place!" But the owner simply replied, "It is still in use and I have no intentions of renting it out." It was such a perfect location and I couldn't just give up that easily. I have confidence only in my determination. ☺ In any case, I persistently called after repeated rejections to plead, "Please, rent it to us! We'll make it into a great place! I beg you!" Finally, around the eighth attempt, the owner caved in and said, "Your enthusiasm wins," and at last, it was ours! Well, there was a rumor that I just happened to have called when he was cheerful and drunk during the New Year celebration... lucky me! ☺

From there, once again I was back to my fundraising days. How many times had I done this already? ☺ This time though, I was discouraged with rightful opinions such as, "How can you ask for money after traveling the world with your wife?" but somehow collected the funds for the property.

Then, with the help of volunteers who saw my homepage, we built everything by hand from the interior to the exterior. On March 31, 2001, the hideout "café-bar & beachside inn BEACH ROCK HOUSE" opened.

With this shop as home base, we plan to continue to add members and create the greatest self-sufficient paradise. So, if anyone is interested, come join us!

more about...ISLAND PROJECT

WEB:
BEACH ROCK VILLAGE
http://www.shimapro.com/

BOOK:
ISLAND STORY • Ayumu Takahashi • One Peace Books

I've lived in Okinawa for only a few years, but I feel that I have, in my own way, learned a great deal from this island.

The words the people of the island use are particularly beautiful. It feels as though the strength and kindness of the people of Okinawa are symbolized. Although they are tender, the words have a sturdy core.

I'd like to share a few of those words and styles of Okinawa, in my words, that I personally like.

What Okinawa Has Taught Me

Word #1: Okinawa
"Yuima-ru"

To tie. Tie together. In other words, to help each other. With harvesting the sugar cane or the work at the sea ports, it's not about "I'll help out, so pay me" but instead it's more like "If you're shorthanded, of course I'll help." And everyone willingly, happily works together. I like that atmosphere.

Word #2: Okinawa
"Chanpuru"

Mix, jam, jumble together. In daily life, it refers to a mixed-up stir-fry dish. At a drinking get-together with young people, it's normal to suddenly realize that there's a baby and a grandmother that's mixed into the crowd, or at a rock band performance, it's not uncommon for a Sanshin (a traditional Okinawa musical instrument) player to join in. The really laid-back attitude of "Oh, forget the little things and let's have a good time together" feels really good.

Word #3: Okinawa
"Nankurunaisa"

The meaning in English might be something like "Don't worry, be happy." Native Americans also teach that there are things that one can control and things that one cannot control. The phrase has a sense of "It's pointless to worry over those things that cannot be controlled! Have a drink and cheer up! The ocean is beautiful again today!" I feel something much deeper because these people have overcome many awful periods of time, including war.

Word #4: Okinawa
"U-maku"

This word means to do something mischievously and without giving up. "U-maku boy" would mean a "mischievous boy." Perhaps something like Tom Sawyer? I want to always be a "U-maku person," laughing off boring common sense, and always cheerfully seeking a new adventure!

Word #5: Okinawa
"Icharibacho-de"

This word means that when people meet, everyone becomes family. Many people of this island are impartial. I feel that they see somebody "as a person" and do not judge based on money or titles. There is a feeling of "what is important is the person who is right here" that drifts in the air of this island. That is probably the reason that it's very easy to meet people here.

Word #6: Okinawa
"chimugurisa"

Normally, when one hears of another's misfortune, words such as "it must be disappointing" or "it must have been difficult" are said in consideration of the person's feelings. But in Okinawa, many people express that as "chimugurisa" (literally meaning: my liver aches, too). Such a feeling toward others, I thought, was wonderful.

Word #7: Okinawa
"niraikanai"

The word indicates "heaven on the other side of the ocean" and has also been translated as "the dragon's palace." Because of an old Okinawa belief that God is on the other side of the ocean, many graves are built facing toward the ocean. Yes, let's all live with our own versions of "niraikanai" in our hearts.

NOW

MY LIFE

-always & forever-
Thirty. My thoughts now.

I finally turned thirty. As I had written up until now—
including that which I could not write about—there was truly
so, so much that happened. But I can say that my twenties
were perfectly satisfying.

If I were to compare my life to the four seasons, I turned
thirty and summer had finally come! And when I turn forty, I
need to give it my all in order to be able to say "my thirties
were completely satisfying."

But, God wouldn't let me take it easy. ☺ The fall after I
turned thirty was a truly serious time. The happiest time and
the most difficult time of my life came at the same time. Two
stories concerning "life" came together.

Late at night on October 1, 2002, I was in the biggest
motorcycle accident of my life. I was in critical condition,
with huge blood loss and ruptured lungs, to the point that
I would have died if I had been rescued ten minutes later.
This accident was not because I drank too much or drove
recklessly, but I was a complete victim of a collision with a
stupid car that ran a red light. As a result, I had broken bones
from head to toe, including my chin, ribs, and both arms. My
lungs and other internal organs had ruptured, and I was in the
ICU for a week, traveling between life and death.

Then, three days after my accident, on October 4, my wife, Sayaka, gave birth to our son, Umi.

She went through delivery in an emotionally and physically worn out state. With her very pregnant belly, she worried whether I was going to live or die while filing the necessary paperwork with the police and hospital. There are no words to express how difficult it must have been for her to be alone at that time. We had wanted a child for so long and we had prepared in so many ways together for this day. Because of that, not being there with her through the birth and heavily burdening Sayaka with everything, I am so angry with myself. "I was really shocked to see you unconscious at the hospital. From that moment on, I kept telling myself that I needed to be strong for you and for our child. I kept thinking that I needed to have patience and the happy, normal days will come back. Oh, but you came back sooner than we thought," she shares with a smile from the kitchen. That fills me with feelings of respect for her from the bottom of my heart right now.

After that, I recovered at a mysteriously fast pace and was discharged from the hospital. Because of my speedy recovery, I was called a "super sayan" in the hospital. ☺ "You're not drinking or injecting something funny on your own, are you?" the doctor asked with all seriousness, and I just had to laugh.

Since the accident, Sayaka has recovered completely from delivery, the baby Umi is happy and healthy, and the three of us are finally able to live together as a family. I am truly nothing but happy.

In hindsight, the month I spent in the hospital was honestly a time of very deep struggles. Although I was unconscious and on the verge of life and death for the first week, when I finally came to, my head and body ached hundreds of times worse than I had imaged. It was truly painful just to be alive, and I came so close to emotionally giving up so many times. I don't know how many times I just wanted to scream, "Kill me now!" lying in the small hospital room with so many IV lines hooked up to me, because I just wanted to escape from the pain all over my body. I don't know how many times I stared at the hospital ceiling on sleepless nights seriously worried that "I'm probably just going to go insane." And there was always the heavy feeling of shame because I could not be there for Sayaka when she needed me the most. I have no recollection of this, but according to friends, I went on a rampage pulling out my IVs and yelling, "I'm going to be with Sayaka and Umi!" I was so violently out of control that the hospital staff had to forcibly inject me with a sedative. At my worst times, I could not control my desire to "escape the person I was at that moment" and was addicted to a very powerful sleeping aid that is only prescribed to those with a serious illness. Seriously, in a sense, it was a legitimate drug addiction.

Faced with a "weak, beaten, and fallen self" that I had never known nor knew could be possible, I got upset and experienced many emotions. Though I can joke about it now, it was truly a period of time when I felt with my entire body what it meant "to live." Oh man, was it a trying month.

My friends, the nurses, the doctors, and of course, my family from back home...many people were consistently and whole-heartedly kind. I truly want to kneel down to those who were so kind. This may be the first time in my life that I have felt this way. Seriously, I thank you. Humans are really incredible. I felt in my heart that I, as a person, was alive because many others had rescued me. I was so moved and cried many tears in that private hospital room.

As every hospital staff had said to me, "It's a miracle you're even alive," I simply believe that there must be another purpose for me to be here. It was a time for me to reacquaint myself with "Ayumu Takahashi" and to gain a new confidence and modesty. Additionally, right now, I strongly and very simply believe that as "a man," I need to once again live decently.

Such is the case, life has it's up and downs, and I am finally beginning to walk again.

Of course the accident was difficult, but I believe the biggest change after turning thirty was the birth of my child. A baby boy we named Umi (meaning ocean). That experience had an overwhelming impression that was a thousand times greater than what I had imagined. It completely changed the way I view life.

Due to the birth of our child, Umi, I am beginning a new relationship with Sayaka, and my concept of what I imagine to be a "cool man" is changing: I am developing a new respect for my mother and father who raised me. I feel somehow as though my range to grow as a person has widened. It feels as though the scenery I can view has gotten bigger.

Standing in the position as a parent to raise a child, I am hit with the reality that I was a baby thirty-eight years ago, and my parents took care of all of my needs. And indeed, I feel indebted to them. Remembering myself back in my young punk days, putting on a front saying, "Parents don't matter. I'm always going to live on my own!" is embarrassing. ☺

So, I turned thirty, became a father, and had a family. I never really imagined me as a father, so honestly, it somehow hasn't become a reality yet. Sometimes, when the three of us are out shopping and I see our reflection in the shop windows, I think, "Wow! We're a family!" It still surprises me. ☺

But family is amazing. Just watching my son, Umi, and my wife, Sayaka, naturally fills my entire body with a core energy of "I'd do anything for them." I think that kind of simple power that appears unconsciously is what puts me into action right now.

I'm slightly embarrassed to say this, but...I believe I love Umi and Sayaka from the bottom of my heart.

As in the past, I hope to always grow as a person as fast as possible, in places I love, with people I love, challenging myself to do the things that I love. Though I do not have any confidence at all in my intelligence, efficiency, or natural-born talents, I do have confidence and determination when it comes to something I love, something I want to do, and I will never give up until it is done.

I, too, am full of painful experiences and bumpy roads with

infinite nights spent without a glimpse of a tomorrow. But at such times, blaming society or others or any number of circumstances and quitting or running away, is lonely. After quitting, it may be easier for a time to blame everything else and acknowledge yourself, but somewhere deep down, loneliness will remain. Instead of ending up like that, I would rather swallow my pride, desperately do everything possible regardless of how painful or difficult, and in the end, share an emotional drink with tears.

Until the day I die, I want to challenge myself with all that I have in everything I want to do. While learning tons from the people around me, I want to nurture myself to be a "big" person to the absolute limit.

Well, let's leave the serious stuff for now.

Simply, this is the only life I have. Let's all, in our own respective paths, challenge ourselves with all that we've got for what we love, laugh, and cry along the way, and grow older. Of course there will be smooth sailing and rough seas, but in the end we have to give it our all.

Tasting fully the joy and the sorrow, I hope we end up as funky old guys and ladies with beautiful smiles. ☺

Be true to the voice in your heart.

one love.

Ayumu Takahashi's

WORDS

Phrases. Thoughts.

"Well, let's first have a drink."

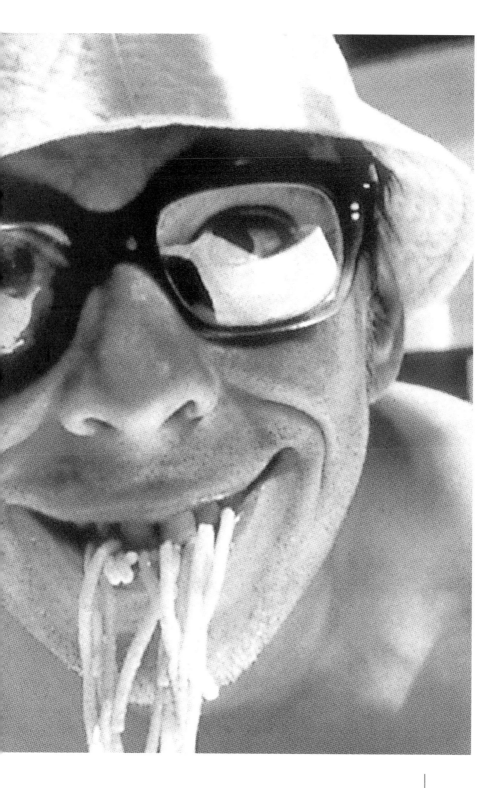

"Isn't Tom Sawyer's world really exciting? The person I admire the most is Tom Sawyer! ☺ While talking with friends, a fun idea comes to mind, we eagerly start planning, 'Yeah! Let's do it!' we decide, and that's how things get started. It's like saying 'Let's cross the river!' or 'Let's build a tree house!' ☺ For me—the bar, the publishing company, the journey around the world, and the island project—everything has been this way. There aren't reasons or a particularly deep meaning to actions."

"Feeling pleasure, happiness, and love; getting goose bumps; and being moved to the point that your entire body shakes; all of those things are not the mind, but what floods unconsciously from the heart. I believe those are our best built-in sensors. I trust those sensors more than anything, so regardless of what others say, I always obey those sensors without hesitation to decide the path of my life."

"Come to think of it, I don't have a life plan. ☺ I always just completely put all of my energy into whatever it is that I want to do at that particular time. Once I accomplish a project, I go back to being nothing and go to various places, do various things, and meet various people, until I encounter that next something that interests me. Then, once again I put all of my energy into that...and I just repeat that process. It seems, for me, that the best standards for decisions in my life are the primitive and simple feelings of 'Wow!' 'Interesting!' and 'Great!'" ☺

"For me, instead of spending an entire life to master one thing, I want to challenge myself with various things guided by my feelings of interest and curiosity. Although I admire craftsmen, I am surely not the type." ☺

adventure life 高橋 歩

"Something like zero to one. There's something I love about that. Perhaps a development fetish? Or an adventure fetish? Yeah, it's something like that. ☺ For whatever reason, in those situations, I am the most passionate. So, when things start to get off the ground, to me, that means 'the end.' I don't know why, but when things start to become stable and are going smoothly, the fun suddenly fades away. In a way, maybe I'm a masochist?" ☺

"Isn't life kind of like the game Dragon Quest? We walk around in various places consulting a map, gather information by talking to people, collect weapons, learn to cast spells, and grow from our experiences. We can choose our own character as well as those of our friends: warrior, soldier, priest, wizard, gambler. In some cases, roles can be changed at the shrine for role changes. And in the end, with the help of friends, the boss is defeated, the princess is saved, and there is peace in the village. Then, on to the next journey...☺ Sometimes, for a split second, I honestly feel as though I am the main character of a game...☺ Of course I live in the real world and have real responsibilities, but there is a part of me that is enjoying life as though it were a game. I really respect the person who created that game."

"What occupation suits me? I haven't given it any thought recently. Instead of choosing an occupation for me from all of the occupations in the world, I just always 'first, do what I want to do, and think about how to make money from it while doing it.'"

"In my case, when I start working on something, I don't think much about whether I'll be able to live off of that or whether it'll be profitable. Always, in the beginning, I do it because I love it. End of story! It's just a matter of working part time or whatever needs to be done in order to live, until I'm able to live off of what I am pouring my heart and soul into. If I chose jobs that were only within the range of 'immediate profit,' my choices would be super slim."

adventure life 高橋 歩

" 'When adults play seriously, it becomes work.' Did you know that law?"

"It's dangerous to misunderstand the phrases 'to have originality' or 'living your life.' They mean that you treasure your sensibility, but it doesn't mean that you don't learn from others. I want to continuously experience, absorb, and learn from the wonderful things filling our world. This life is a one and only in this world anyway, so of course it's going to be original and personal." ☺

"I was often told by other adults, 'You guys are all talk,' since the age of about twenty. Well, of course. You can only talk about it in the beginning. Results and accomplishments come later. First, you just have to give it your all with that baseless confidence."

"First, there has to be self-satisfaction. And when you keep pursuing deep down into that self-satisfaction, I think it naturally becomes something that reaches others."

"If giving my absolute all to do something that I love can support just one other person's happiness, it makes my day. If I could live my life that way, it would be the best."

"It's useless to do anything that I don't like. I suddenly become nervous and spineless. And I easily get stomachaches...☺ Therefore, I believe I should choose what I like in the first place. I believe I do a good job because it's something I enjoy, and doing a good job is helpful for many people."

"Until I was starting my own bar when I was twenty, I had never taken on a big challenge. I had never seriously attempted anything that seemed impossible to me. But when I survived that experience, for the first time in my life, I had confidence in myself."

"When I was twenty and went into serious debt to get the money to open a bar, and I stacked the 6.2 million yen before my eyes...my stomach knotted up for the first time. Until that moment, we were high on just doing it, but when I saw the cash, I remember feeling scared (as in, this is for real now...). All because we'd heard so many stories about people wasting their lives from debt or others that had committed suicide over debt. But at that time, there wasn't a choice of going back, so we just had to drink and laugh away our worries and fear."

"When I was twenty-two, with four bars and the media attention on us, our friends and the world treated us as great heroes. I was surprised at the praise from the world, but I was also surprised at how conceited I had become. Because before I knew it, I had become that kind of person I never wanted to be." ☺

"I'm stupid, so when something starts to go right, I become arrogant and have a habit of becoming big-headed quickly. I have to be careful. If I start to look down on something, even a tiny bit, I lose sight of the important things and my growing as a person slows down. But as always, God says 'Grow more! Become a bigger man!' and sends new teaching materials my way, so I shouldn't even have time to be conceited."

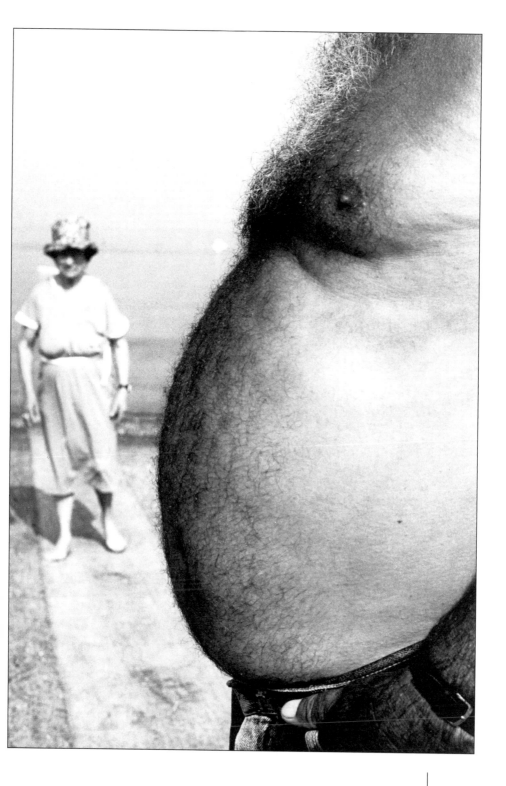

サカナおやじ

"Forever be humble!"

ニョ□坊

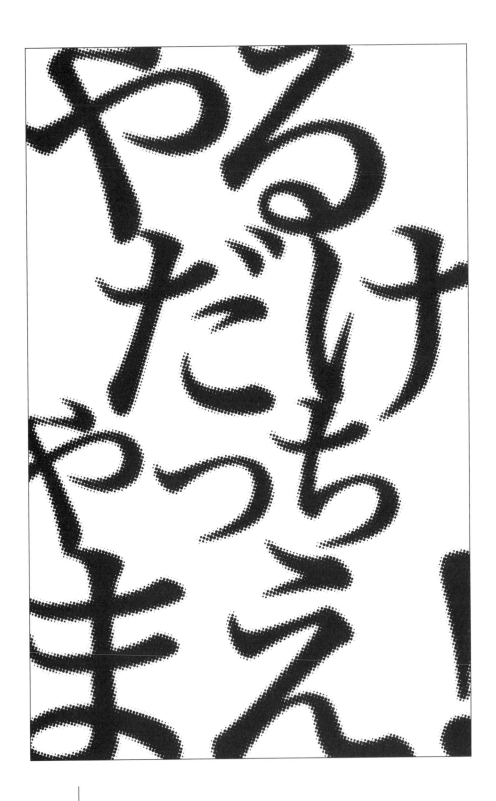

やるなら
やるだけ
やっちまえ!
もちろん!

"Huh? You want to start your own shop? Do it! Do it! ☺ Well, what you need is really simple. First, acquire the necessary skills and knowledge, find a venue, gather funds, build the shop, and go! Just like that. Nothing moves forward if you think complicated, so keep your mind simple and actions powerful."

"Once I have a goal, I just try everything that comes to mind, without thinking too much and start moving. At first, it's a game of physical strength. ☺ With what I feel at that moment in that situation as a base while I am in action, I can come up with a strategy for the future. Everything can't go as planned anyway, so instead of worrying before you begin, I think why not worry as you go. I still like the sense of 'First, just do it! Give it your all!'

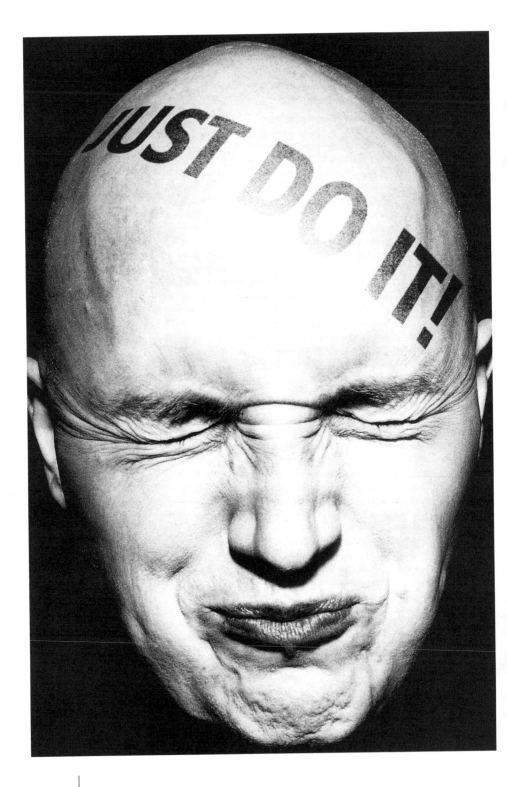

"Worry? Fear? Anxiety? I have them always, of course. But I'll do it anyway." ☺

"I'm good at pretending not to be scared. ☺ There isn't anybody who isn't scared of something, right? I just think the biggest difference is whether you do it even though you're scared, or you quit because you're scared."

"Dimming the heart is my worst fear. It is admirable to always be dignified, but life seems boring when the heart stops feeling. If anything, I want to continue to be amazed, confused, and shaken." ☺

"Whenever I work with friends, I always tell myself 'Pushing away is also love. Not assisting is also love.' Though I am often in a position of a leader or a representative, I am not their parents, but am their friend to the end. I would rather grow with them instead of teaching or improving them."

"Needless to say, friends are important. But I don't think 'I first need to make friends...' or 'I need to keep the pace with my friends...' I always take that first step thinking that 'I can do this on my own' regardless of how hard the headwinds are blowing. And I think, on the contrary, that I become friends with those who have these intentions themselves."

"Regardless of the fact that you work hard together with friends, in the end, you are different human beings. It's only natural for each individual to think, decide, act, and take responsibility for oneself. And a group that strangely understands and forgives one another is scary." ☺

"If everyone voices their true opinions, even if that causes an argument, we can move forward. But it seriously makes me sick to my stomach when I see people talking negatively or putting someone down behind their back. I don't ever want to be that jackass that bad-mouths his friends."

"In my thirty years of life, I have not yet despaired or failed in the true sense. I feel as though that has become a type of inferiority complex for me. I feel that 'I will never truly understand the feelings of those who are really in pain or are suffering...' Well, there's nothing I can do about it."

"It is always the same pattern—for the bar, for the publishing company, and even this time for the Island Project. Whenever we—the penniless, inexperienced, and connectionless—started something, the people around us had a lot to say: the economy is this or that, independence should come after many years of training, the real world is tough, don't underestimate the business world. Well, surely, they are right. ☺ But interestingly enough, their reactions immediately change when things start going even a little well after getting over our initial mistakes. They'd boast, 'I knew you'd do it,' or 'that advice was useful after all, wasn't it?' and some would even say 'I taught him everything he knows.' ☺ What outsiders say is unreliable. Seriously, there's no need to mind even a micron of it."

"In a sense, the beginning is always a failure and reflection fetishism. ☺ In other words, things don't just start off perfect. That's impossible. Why would an amateur succeed from the beginning? Think of the debt in the beginning as tuition. Just think that one day it'll make a great story. In short, 'when you fall, fall forward.' If you're not successful at first, don't run, hang in there, and a complete victory in the end is all that matters."

"I long for something, try it, fail, try again, fail again, try yet again, fail yet again, times a hundred million...and succeed in the end with an emotional drink! It's always like that. ☺ Two steps forward one step back? Don't kid yourself. It's more like one hundred million falls!"

| *adventure life* 高橋 歩

"Possibility isn't zero, so let's give it a go!"

"When it's really time to fight, I try to not think of anything and face it straight on. Of course if I lose, I will be disappointed, but it feels better that way regardless of the outcome. It would be terrible to lose as a result of using tricks after complicatedly thinking through everything. I wouldn't be able to sleep for three days." ☺

"If all the geniuses were on top of the world by the age of three, then it might be easier to give up and say 'There's a difference in natural born talents. It's impossible for me...' But surprisingly, there are many that were brought up in an average environment. When I learn of such things, I get fired up and think 'Damn it. Why, I can do it too.' It's easy to blame your immaturity on your lack of talent for everything, but I don't care for stuff like that. For example, it's as simple as the fact that while we were playing Nintendo as kids, Ichiro desperately practiced batting. I believe we can all be geniuses if it's something we love."

"In daily life, regardless of how busy I am, I take half an hour everyday as time for being 'a person.' It's free time, closing the door completely to the daily responsibilities of work. I make such time to just veg in order to look over my life. It's not to think about today or tomorrow, but to take time in looking at the big picture of my life. In doing so, 'now' begins to seem even dearer, and sometimes there is a moment when the center of my sensitivity gently rises. I truly believe that time like this may be what creates me as a person."

"I consciously make an effort to always keep a clear mind. Anytime my mind starts to get even remotely jumbled, I head to a relaxing café with a notebook and pen in hand. Having myself a nice glass of ice coffee, I ask myself, 'What's the problem, exactly? And so, what am I going to do? What do I want to do?' It's become a habit to organize my thoughts in this way by jotting down the answers in my notebook. Because, people with an organized, simple mind have powerful actions, right? I want to be that way, too."

"There is an 'observation self' within me that objectively sees myself. For example, if I am running a marathon, I get tired and think 'I can't do this. I want to quit.' Then my other self says 'You're going to quit because it's tough, huh?' Then I think 'Of course not!' ☺ I'm always having conversations like this with myself. Is that kind of dangerous?" ☺

"Why not roam the world?"

| *adventure life*　高橋 歩

"Something I felt while I traveled the world was that people living where there is nothing, such as in Africa with only desert or in Mongolia with only plains, have smiles filled with happiness and unbearably friendly faces. They display emotions with their entire bodies. It felt as though they exchanged with others what their bodies felt, expressing with their whole body exactly as they felt it. It was straightforward and pleasant; as a human being, I thought it was attractive. Standing on African land, I thought with self-hatred 'Wow, I'm somehow tainted...'" ☺

"Meeting people that were living simply and comfortably while I traveled the world made me feel as though 'I was carrying a lot of baggage in life that was unnecessary.' I began to feel that I also needed not to protect many things, but I wanted to gracefully choose and deeply love the really important things."

"If you think in simple terms, humans may be happy enough with only food, sleep, and love. Perhaps our lives have become too complicated."

| *adventure life* 高橋 歩

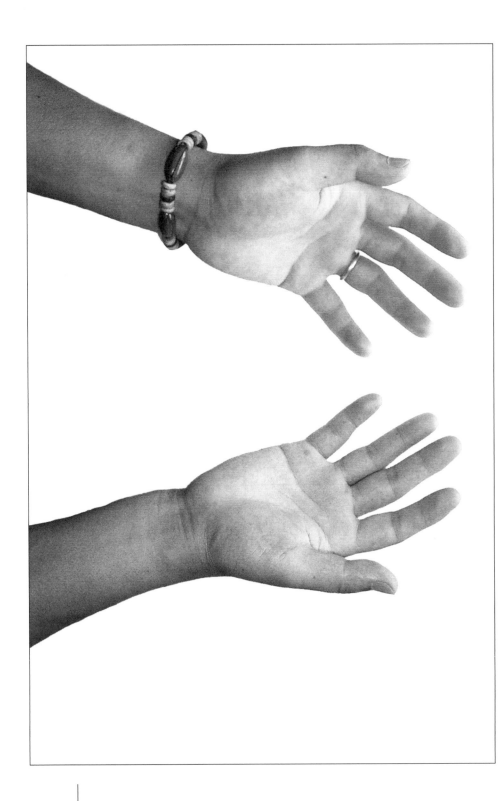

"You choose everything."

"I love Sayaka's face when she smiles. Before making jumbled statements, I will start by making this woman happy."

"There are good times and bad times in work. The same goes for health. Appearances change, aspirations might change, and even personalities may change. But I married the person I honestly yearned for in the center of my heart, the 'person I want to live this life with to the end.'"

"

"A guy who can't make his own woman happy, can't possibly make Japan or the earth happy."

"I love my parents. I seriously believe that both of them were my greatest teachers. Therefore, I yearn to be praised by them and to meet their expectations. I always have, even from back in the old days of being a punk."

"My mother was the type of parent who always asked at the dinner table, 'Ayumu, did anything good happen today? Anything fun?' As an elementary school kid, I felt pressured to answer her. But because I grew up always hearing those questions, I believe I naturally developed an antenna to pick up on fun and interesting things."

"Recently, I visited my parents for the first time in a while, shared a drink with my father, and was surprised. Because, my father was saying the same sort of things that I say at my talk shows. Moreover, the wording was even exactly the same. Until now, I'd thought that I'd created my own way of thinking, but I realize that in the end, I was very influenced by my parents. I realized that I was this person's son, after all. In that sense, we may never be able to surpass our parents." ☺

"While I traveled the world and even living in Okinawa, when spending time surrounded by overwhelming beauty, my body simply overflows with the feeling that 'the earth is amazing! It's beautiful to be alive!' and without reason I feel happy. I believe from the very core of my being that I must save them for when my children are adults."

"Really admirable people pour their love out to each individual around them, not just limited to their spouses and children. Family, siblings, friends, lovers, people who have taken care of you...it's surprisingly difficult to really treasure those who are truly important to you."

"The toughest guys are the most gentle and kindest. I want to be that way, too."

"It's not all…me, me, me. First, it's about accepting the other person's rhythm, and then gradually blending in together. It's a unique dimension that the people of Okinawa possess. I don't yet have enough of that." ☺

adventure life 高橋 歩

"Seeing Sayaka happy makes me happy. Not just limited to Sayaka, but when I feel that something I did makes someone happy or my work has benefited someone, that may be the best happiness. It's often said that happiness makes people happy. It's true, happiness is connected."

"Choosing something means abandoning something else.
Loving someone means not loving someone else. It looks like
I still lack the courage to choose."

| *adventure life* 高橋 歩

"We create ourselves. What part of ourselves we foster changes our future. See ourselves and our lives as a creation. I like that point of view."

adventure life 高橋 歩

"Learn until death. That is an important promise I have made with myself."

"I don't want to protect the present self but to continue to change. I want to continue to exchange the old self for a new self and be reborn over and over again. I only need to treasure for life what naturally remains, regardless of how many times I change."

| *adventure life*　高橋 歩

"Do not bear the present for the future, but enjoy living the present for the future."

"Have big dreams? Living your own way of life? It doesn't matter. Whether you have big dreams or not, whether you are living your own way of life or not, in the end, I believe that the one who enjoys life is the strongest. Ultimately, I just want to enjoy life every day."

| *adventure life* 高橋 歩

"Freedom and happiness are not something to become, but rather something to be felt. More through my skin. More and more through my body. I want to value my own sensitivity."

"Life is to be enjoyed."

| *adventure life* 高橋 歩

"Everything begins while sharing a drink, but dreams don't come true by just drinking! ☺ All right, let's do our best again tomorrow!"

Epilogue
Note from the Author

This time, in creating this book, I took a look at the thirty years of my life. Frankly, I was hit with an overwhelming feeling that Ayumu Takahashi has a ways to go, and oftentimes I was somewhat embarrassed. But I believe that I have poured all that I possibly could into this book.

Now, life's true stage begins. Life is limited. The time I have left is limited. At best, life is eighty years. What one person can do, physically and mentally, is limited. Those limits cannot be removed by anyone. Therefore, I believe I must try my hardest to simply do what I desire.

How can I have the best life possible within that time limit? This is the theme at my roots.

I do not know what I will be reborn as the next time, but in this life, I was born as a son to Gen and Keiko Takahashi, in this country of Japan, and in this generation. My years have been spent with my brother Minoru, my sister Miki, and many friends. I met and married the woman, Sayaka, and I have been blessed with my son, Umi. And now, I am here.

I would not be here now if even one person had been missing. I am sincerely grateful to those important people. Thank you so much.

And I hope to live my life naturally, loving those that love me forever and ever.

And lastly, it is a sort of fate that we have met through this book. While walking our respective paths freely, wouldn't it be interesting if one day our lives intersected!

Until we meet again.

A life (journey) of freedom with the ones you love.

Have a nice trip!!
Ayumu Takahashi
Summer, 2010 in Okinawa, Japan

Presented by A-Works
Ayumu Takahashi & Good Fellows.